ALTERLIFE

WRITTEN BY MILO PRATHER

ILLUSTRATED BY SAULI RAUHALA

*To those chained by their ghosts—you
are stronger than their whispers.*

TABLE OF CONTENTS

Canine and the Core *(3)*   12

Wolfwalker *(2)*   13

Tundra Aurora   14

Maritime to Mountain Time   16

Lake of Lost Love   18

Ramblings *(1)*   19

Scarification   20

Stratification   21

Ghost   22

Voyager   24

Gold Rush   25

Misty   26

Flurry   27

Excoriation *(1, 2, 3)*   28

Thanatophobia *(1, 2, 3)*   29

Eat Your Young *(1, 3)*   30

Hellhound's Maw *(3, 4, 5)*   32

Aphonia *(2, 4, 5, 6, 7)*   34

Rinse and Repeat *(3, 4, 5, 6)*   35

The Episode *(4, 5, 6)*   36

Musings of the Christmas Past *(2, 3, 4, 5)*   38

Musings of the Christmas Present *(4, 5)*   40

Musings of the Christmas Future *(2, 3)*   42

Civil Twilight   44

Astronomical Twilight   45

Arctic Circle of Fire   46

Storytelling   47

Lean Into   48

Nightfire   49

Author's Note   50

* Refer to next page for specific trigger warnings (1-7)

You are never alone.

Trevor Lifeline
text 678678 or dial (866) 488-7386

National Domestic Violence Hotline
text 88788 or dial (800) 799-7233

RAINN National Sexual Assault Hotline
text 64673 or dial (800) 656-4673

Suicide and Crisis Lifeline
dial 988

updated 12-14-2025

TRIGGER WARNINGS

Please read at your own discretion. This book contains content that may be triggering for some audiences, including mentions of:

(1)   Self-harm tendencies

(2)   Suicidal ideation

(3)   Blood/graphic imagery

(4)   Sexual assault

(5)   PTSD/flashbacks

(6)   Coercion

(7)   Arachnophobia

THE CANINE AND THE CORE

Heartwood ablaze, this slow violence, I am wanted dead or alive.
The world burns around me, in me—my cinder coat, paws of ash,
muzzle agape with a cry, *run for your life*. It approaches, time slips
away from us; reflections of hopeless love are scalding blisters.

Evergreen mother, she who once stood tall,
diseased and gray, her neighbor aflame
both don their shriveled roots;
we began this disturbance long ago.

A creature escaping a forest,
the flames lick and nip
at a terror-tucked tail;
escaping, or trapped?

Pack animals,
we disconnected
from our instinct.

It was only meant
to be a dying fire.

How long was it
until the spark
was thrown
tooth and
claw, crash
and teeter
beginning
the clock
and the
end of
the
last

regime.

WOLFWALKER

A hot morning in the western Wyoming sun, Rawhide Coffee for my tired eyes; sitting at a high-table with a latte in hand, I greet the versions of myself left to the lands.

Who I am, everything I am meant to be, it is dormant in the petrified trees and sulfuric slopes—time stands still in Yellowstone. With each turn of Dunraven Pass, I become more familiar with my wilderness; from the fires to the storms, to the floods and the muds, to a wolf trotting his way along a midsummer-green trail.

I throw on the brakes as he approaches the road and pauses to stare. Is he looking at me?

Green-fire eyes. He's *watching* me.

We are curious about each other, though meant to walk different realms; we part ways, me in my blue Subaru and him up his juniper trail. *This*, I realized, *is my survival*—my breath of life on the verge of death, lone-wolf tendencies do not serve my instinctual heart. He and I, we both knew what it meant to be a pack animal.

I hiked to see the Yellowstone River that afternoon, and though she was once cruel, the force of this land taught me how to overcome my fears of disaster; lesson and love will always exist amidst the chaos. I thanked the river for the floods of change; I forgave her for teaching me that the most beautiful forms of life are as dangerous as they are admirable.

TUNDRA AURORA

I've learned the art of chasing the aurora
desperate to spark the feeling of *home*
grasping for the light of the north
alike in my heart
as to the skies

like a wolf to its prey
retracing the cycle
the steps of elk
rewinding time
into the tundra
restructuring
the balance
in my nature

12,000 ft:
I sit underneath the stars
scowling at the light pollution
from the city in the distance,
so I search the skies
for a flicker of reassurance
in this hushed alpine.
A few glimpses of hope,
a flare of a green hue,
and a jacket from Alaska Seaplanes.

"Watch it appear in the canyon on the way *home*, to laugh at us,"

I say,
racing down
mountain to canyon
I slam on my brakes
aside the river
who somehow
led me to the north

her freshly burnt ponderosas
hiding in the shadows
of the midnight mountains

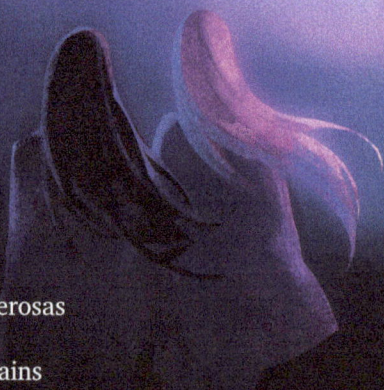

pink light spreads a blanket
underneath the stars
a green wave
between her jagged peaks
crashing *home*

blood luminescent
throbbing vessel
flare of my sun
and I am
pulled
back
to
the
fjords
mossy trails
misty rainforests
gentle rain on rock

I ease my foot off the pedal
and I realize I am in no rush
not anymore, at least—

time bent like a ray in the eve
home lies on its continuum
interlaced atmosphere to space
everything is always connected

I must twist the wheel
backward
forward
weaving
behind the stars
in my eyes
ribbons of memory
pink and green;

my roots are failing to thrive in permafrost.

MARITIME TO MOUNTAIN TIME

I am timeless:
split between two realities
I curse the Universe
for showing me a reflection
of my ghost in the glass

Hands stiff and swollen
damp autumn air sinking
into the handle of a squeegee
skeletons of bugs
on the windshield
first light dew
on the windows
street to dock

A limb stuck in the same motion—
top down, left to right
the recall and the retreat
toss the rain, the soap, aside
to gasoline-infested concrete
or oil-slick salt water

Once in the gray clouds
through a fog amongst the fjord;

Balancing above
cold Pacific water
holding a frozen boat rail
close to my heart

Twice in the light of the gas station
on the corner of two silent roads;

On the tightrope
of sane and stuck
binding my body
against a rumbling engine

Alaska;
the clock wanes
frost blankets grass
skin frozen to boat rail
morning darkness unveils
the moon's face stealing me
from home

Colorado;
worn patience
hesitant mornings
thick wildfire smoke
a bent smile like the pine
makeup to disguise tired eyes
from home

Both, it will fade—
bug guts into the street
and dew drops on the dock
the ghost of my memory
haunts my becoming
to parallel mirrors

I am timeless:
wisps of the present, the past, the path
maritime to mountain time
pink skies at night, sailor's delight
red sun at morning, forester's warning

LAKE OF LOST LOVE

Through the sheen of mist in the rainforest
I watched the echoes of my past
envelope the hemlock and spruce
and all of their skeleton trunks

Struggling up the mountain
calves burning and chest heaving
I choke down the emotions haunting me
heartbreak so familiar
yet without a face

A pond of old water sat at the top of the trail
a mist of raw open-wound droplets
the new rain hushing the forest

My jaw caught in its path
forming a half-understood explanation:

A lake of my own pooling emotions
my past memories
lost love
pelted with droplets anew

I slid and tumbled down through the woods
brushing against the Devil's Club
gathering moss and thorns
I am balanced against all odds of wet soil

I was rushing to therapy
collecting parts of the earth on my sleeve
washing myself with the rain who promised
a whisper of healing
I ran from the old growth

DESERT RAMBLINGS

Through the haze of sand in the desert
I tread barefoot atop cacti and peridot
grasping onto wavering apprehension
for the illusion of respite

With these sunburns and scarred blisters
a sickly shape with ribs protruding
I plead the water for a taste of heaven
hallucinatory heat waves
parch my purpose

In the arid drought I ramble the dunes
holy water meeting cracked lips
a desert echoing with coarse screams

With a collapsing fate
I am withering away:

In this arc of pain
I would sit through a hurricane
and not drink a droplet
if it meant saving your parched body

There is no rescue in this expanse
I have never willed for this storm
yet I sit begging for my tears back
motionless in the quicksand I created

Strike me down again
I will wing my way alone
dehydrating with each salty shed tear
my final lick of fight
I survive for the hope of paradise

SCARIFICATION

I am but a fleck

of my becoming

layers too serried

to crawl from carapace

before my legacy

scar my skin

for I cannot grow

without your abrasion

trust me, please—I must be split open
before I can prove my heights.

STRATIFICATION

Umbos ward against haste
finger-pricking brood
guarded from foreign touch
ill with the force of souls ~~hungry~~
addicted
to her majesty's fortitude;

the giant's tiny seed
between its fortress of bracts
alone, crushed underfoot
enclose her in a ribcage
armed and guarded
with shields habitually blacksmithed
for a heart sharp to the touch.

Guard it, do not break me open—

I am but a whisper of life
barely kept safe
by my repetitive destruction.

With the delicate and deciduous
a little more and a little less than *evergreen*
the spin of time's cycle
will crack the cone, it begins;

rebirth must be serotinous.

GHOST

carrying nature and nurture
transparent skin
attached to the spirit of an entity
alive with spite
death will not take me

weaving direction
between phantom limbs
the river and rapture
of a beating heart
fingertips surrender
to the soil and the stars

an ethereal and earthen companion
to the ghost of a woman's womb
I am sewn together by two parts
functioning as a whole
in this scorched landscape

deliver my voice
and fasten hand to heart

VOYAGER

beneath the frames of boundless pines

the stare of an apparition

shadows the wing

of a free passenger

a heavenly canvas

construed by recast wilderness

somber solitude within

the thunderstorm harmonizes

with songs of married ancients

a cruel curse for a river

meant to settle

between canyon crevices

of reminiscence

and to slip away

would be his surmise

for his milk marrow

dissolves with rainpour

the canopy failed to veil

GOLD RUSH

Day 2—Deep Lake Camp

With each mile I carry my fifty-pound backpack, I am more aware of the agony it brings to my body; yet, with the promise of repose, I become blinded to my baggage.

A clear water stream blocked us from our tent site—it rained last night, crossing stones submerged amongst rushing water. I chose to hike in XtraTuffs for all 33 miles of this trail, an intriguing decision considering their complete lack of grip and ankle support. *But,* I am an Alaskan deckhand, in the same shoes I remain upright against six-foot waves.

I did not hesitate to navigate the moss-slicked rocks. It wasn't graceful. My feet got a bit wet, *sure,* but it could've been a lot worse (the rain boots were a tactical choice). My hiking companions, quietly laughing at my audacity, commented on my willpower to traverse the rushing creek while carrying so much weight; my burden was forgotten in the shadow of conquering an obstacle.

I do not fear the precarious despite my heavy traumas, capable of ignoring all odds as long as I am promised a place of rest.

MISTY

There exists a cure in the fog blanketing the trees of the valley, I
blindly wander toward haze-hidden paths.

Between the clarity and confusion of a hushed earthbound cloud,
lapping up the tears of the pines; this sweet sorrow is my elixir, a
panacea to my purpose.

The ways of natural medicine and new love, of healing from the
white whispers of the trees—

I have learned to love what I will lose.

FLURRY

A bath of the new from the old processes of this earth; the trees bear heavy snow and drink its weight come spring.

To take the winter with grace, to let their branches bend to the burden of the storms, to wait for the warmth to melt away the heft—time will nourish my roots.

Letting go with easc is my libation.

EXCORIATION

To relish the sweet savor of death's
desperation and temptation; it is a heat
unfamiliar in this riparian landscape, an
anomaly, an outlier, this wetland of sapidity
spits out the soot of my ghosts.

I did not miss this feeling, the blistered body
and obsessive mind, it roars against the
gentle whisper of pines and birdsong; all but
a craving for nothingness, an excuse of a fire
retardant.

I'm fighting harder, tearing off my tongue and
scraping away my taste buds, for I will do
anything to avoid the taste of death.

THANATOPHOBIA

I am equally afraid of death's touch as much
as I crave its comfort; numbness of
nothingness, silence of the soil's embrace,
ashes rushing with rapids.

Standing in this river alive: thanatophobia,
they call it, my life ahead gleams with
uncertainty's hope, the terror of knowing I
left a moment too early.

I fight with everything in me, hostile to this
pain, petrified of my scythe—I refuse to lose
this battle to my own front lines.

EAT MY YOUNG

Destruction, I crave,
these wounds are infectious,
I feast on naivety
and lick the blood off its bones.

Must I remove
this sanguinity
to survive?

I am obsessed with restarting,
frailty and fortress;
a disembowled wraith
with its limbs
in the clutch of canines.

I have been raised
to compete in my own ring,
deathmatches
are in my nature.

I am ready for new brood
to tear heart from chest;
devour my spirit
for he is my runt.

HELLHOUND'S MAW

I race at my memories
with an open jaw
eager for a fresh kill;
a beast with red eyes,
a snarl that frightens the bear.

Saliva dripping from canines
stained in red,
my tongue lashing
with the delicacy
of demon-borne blood.

I lunge at his throat,
scrape at his chest,
tear out his flesh.

Oh, how sweet blood tastes
when tainted with justice,
your family cannot save you now.

Beneath my claws, his beating heart
raw with the intention
to end my life.

I dive my muzzle through his ribcage;
in the latch of my jaws
a heart still pounding,
and how savory it is—

to

stop

it.

Pause its rhythm,
he carves scars into my breast
a mistake: a sigil in disguise
quietly, unleash the wolf.

In my maw is his intention,
burning alive
flicker of the flame of fury,
I am not your hellhound.

APHONIA

Coarse gray fabric digs welts around my neck, to speak
or not to speak; undecided, warped words on twisted
tongue.

Distended, I cannot mouth *no*.

I retch with the contamination between worth and
death, *limbo* is the bathroom of spiders, *split* is my
hoarse voice usurped to the glare of blue eyes.

I am the in-between of a healed and wide-open wound,
skin ripping in the purgatory of a sandpaper couch.

*Your living resistance
is better off dead.*

RINSE AND REPEAT

This year, Halloween called me back to the dead within my own walls, I had carefully crafted a costume to cater to the craters in my heart—I perform in a black veil and bright red lipstick, obsessive over how tight I can bind the corset.

I invited someone to the party, we'd gone on a couple dates before. He forces a drink into my hand. I swallow my booze and shudder at a foreign hand rubbing my thigh. *It must be my PTSD.* Loud and friendly, that's all.

I escape to the bathroom with my roommate, needing distraction. A shadow in the bright vanity lights, I am a time traveler; my mouth is on my roommate's chest to evade the threat outside, the bathroom is infested with spiders.

Anger whispers beyond the door and pulls me back to lips I don't belong to; *I said no, I said stop.* He hands me another drink, barely drunk himself, groping me as I stumble to my roommate's room. I hold them close with terror trapping me in shivers, we tumble onto the floor, my knee is between their legs, I was sobbing naked in their bed two years ago—this is safe sexuality.

But I am still haunted, a crying mess of a woman, my voice splits when I mention coercion. We kick him out, the party ends abruptly because of me. I am dizzy in his haze of sex jokes.

Raw and stripped bare in the searing shower that dowses me with the last of my worth, I cannot scrub my skin enough to rid me of my guilt. I am stuck in this landmine of war and love—and, I wonder, if it is hope that I am washing down the drain.

THE EPISODE

This, I thought, must be impossible.

I cannot help but wonder—how, if it terrifies me,

do I worry so much about losing it?

Sickened I am, my past chases me down in the
daylight; every part of me is stained with the ink
of past lovers warping the words of my story.

He still crawls underneath my skin.

I trust him. Him. *Him*.

Seventeen. He begged me to cry for him.
Vulnerability, I guess. Something like that.
We're on the couch next to my room while my
mother's voice echoes downstairs. He smiles as
my tears dampen his shirt where my head lays
upon his chest. He starts to cry, I cradle his jaw
in my palm, I stifle my anguish and swallow my
pain. I comfort him. He matters, not I. His hand
slips underneath the blanket.

The room darkens. It burns. Tightened
shoulders. Rigid body. Fast breaths. Blurry
vision. Ears ringing.

Where am I?

"Do you want someone to talk to?" he asks
me, blue scrubs and wet hair, a styrofoam cup
of hot tea in his hands. "No pressure, though."

I nod. He sits next to me. Caught, or noticed?
My body is frozen to the chalkboard in the
corner, knees pulled to my chest, a tremoring
voice, swollen and sore eyes. I don't
understand why I'm letting him in. My pain
spills from my mouth, I am a mess of who I
once was. His voice is gentle, new. Genuine.
His legs are pointed in his chair toward me.
He's practicing the art of listening.

                                        Afraid to cry,

day three.

                    Forgotten scenes creep up in the dark of the
                       night on the brink of sleep. I cannot trust a
                          man, I haven't since then. My mind and
                                        body are at war,

I am understood.

                              It all started with you, didn't it?

And it's ending with him.

                                              the end,

for the beginning.

MUSINGS OF THE CHRISTMAS PAST

I have become more comfortable in the discomfort
of green-wired lights pulled from an old red bin;
it is approaching—my scars lay hidden
in the smell of the cinnamon wax burner
and fresh fir sap sticking to my fingertips,
shadows of twisted words: long hands: sharp nails
lurking behind the pots and pans in the kitchen
where a reflection of festive light
outlines a haunted house
dirty with philosophy.

Underneath the veil of holiday jolly
woven together by the frigid cold,
I fight in a war of memory and time;
a clash of pain and pleasure on Thanksgiving Day,
convulsing on my bedroom floor
moans escape my lips at the sensation of his weight
and the lingering licks of sweet potato pie lay
underneath the taste of his mouth.

I stumble across his favorite quote:

"I am naturally warlike.
Attacking is one of my instincts."

- Nietzsche

I grasp for control, reach for my armor,
yet I wander downstairs to don a fabricated smile
because the control I so desperately crave
is not but a barrel to my forehead,
a loaded gun of invisible bullets;
I didn't mean to, I *swear*, I didn't want to read it,
I am only 18 as time's continuum bends,
I am only a stranger to these old ghosts.

A one-man soldier in a blood-smeared battlefield
of snowmen and angels and nutcrackers
a confused and dizzy wine-drunk escapist
holding a hand of cards I can never play right,
an intoxicated standing statue of shed skin
"Everything will be okay when you return home,"
a hazy buzz whispers to me, the clock strikes midnight,
I tell it to listen closely, because I *am* home,
I am *home*, a shadow in the bathroom mirror.

My survivor's instinct stares back at me,
donning her graduation robe and weapon of words—
I'd survived without knowing the threat;
time freezes with the winter winds in Kansas
so I will fight with the forces of my fears
for the hope of memories easing steady,
and while I peer into a glass ornament
I finally catch a glimpse
of who I really am.

My favorite poem has never changed:

*"The phoenix hope
can wing her way through the desert skies
and still defying fortune's spite
revive from ashes and rise."*

- *Miguel de Cervantes Saavedra*

MUSINGS OF THE CHRISTMAS PRE

MUSINGS OF THE CHRISTMAS PRESENT

I have become more comfortable in the discomfort of the ghosts who shackle me each winter.

My frigid chains drag across the Atlantic, my gravestones are far behind; here, I tread softly upon the resting grounds of my ancestors and heed their warnings. Body cradled by snow beside a silent frozen lake, I plead the giants to free me—these demons attached to my heart long ago.

I am a medium of sorts, barely able to communicate with the apparitions that bind my wrath to body. Their shadows sit at the table where I write and possess my shaking hands—it begins.

This time, I do not face my deadly curse alone, I am armed and allied. I cannot write, tormented; I am there again, I never told him yes, I am begging for respite.

Is it defeat I feel when I finally lay to rest upon another shoulder?

I am a fallen soldier again; fingers tangling in hair, I can't breathe, my army waves their white flags. The sound of a man's voice, I banished that old memory, I have changed. My tears are shared, I am at last telling the stories of the times I bled out on the battlefield.

This pain, it is not lonely.

I am here, I am safe—Thanksgiving is far away. Tonight, we will relax together after work, a quiet celebration of gratitude with Juleøl and Swedish meatballs. Thankful is all I can be today, this moment in time where I at last break from the entities; they have always belonged in the afterlife, anyway.

This paper is the present. I've rewritten this story day after day, draft by draft; what it means to exist in the moment, my hand holds this fickle heart of mine. I live in these lines, to cry away ghosts I exorcise with ink and pen, this is how I will wing my way, I am reviving from ashes.

I will rise again.

MUSINGS OF THE CHRISTMAS FUTURE

I am standing at the foot of my grave.

Something must change for me to live.

The future is never set in stone.

A return to the cemetery

is my fight to alter my fate.

I WILL NOT LOSE MY WAR TO DEATH'S GRASP.

CIVIL TWILIGHT

In this blue-walled kitchen, I'm watching a romance movie while making dinner, though I'm constantly distracted with checking the current KPI; it's a new obsession of mine, chasing the aurora, though I have yet to learn why I'm so drawn to the light of the north.

A fire alarm beeps down the road, faint. A young girl screams. I'm alert, I'm awake.

Sirens don't follow, my heart eases. The fire department is on the end of our street in this 24-block town. I hear a child's laugh; someone must've burned a treat. For a moment, my inner child pushes against my ribcage. She's responding to the girl's joy. I set down my spatula—

—*the obsession,* it's from her.

I take off running down the Alaskan streets and abandon my dinner, wearing my pajamas and a big sherpa jacket; I stand still in the Alabama summer as I compare a book of constellations to the sky above, wishing for a shooting star. I am shouting about the faint green glow in the evening sky; I am begging my father to set up his telescope in the porchlight of a borrowed base home. I am jumping into my roommate's navy blue Wrangler to chase the northern lights; I am pressing my face to the windows in my father's army green Compass on a warm southern night to peer at Mars far above us.

Both, the horizon lingers at dusk and promises my path ahead; with the collision of time and polaris, I carry the hope of civil twilight's guiding star.

ASTRONOMICAL TWILIGHT

Sundown in the north follows its winter curse as my time here shortens, dwindling safety impelling my obsession with the clock and calendar. Navigating the shadows of a familiar lifetime, caught in the inevitable cycle: my cemetery awaits me, but I am a stranger to nyctophobia.

I savor each second of daylight with the ache of knowing I will soon slip between the valleys of the uncertain dark, a future foggy with flurries of the familiar unknown. My eyes sting with the last of the northern sunrays splitting the clouds of an incoming snowstorm; I chase the minutes backward on ice-slicked sidewalks, I am desparate to revel in time's tortuous flow.

My tears blur the sight of dusk falling upon mountain peaks; the break of day will soon become a memory of dawn. Often we value the light only when it flees us—gratitude becomes my lantern as night falls, I am blinded by its flame and bathe in its warmth. This is my respite, this is my rest, how much must I thank the sun, how much must I beg the moon?

I cannot escape this revolution.

The solstice will remind me that all is temporary, the light and dark and all their faces, there is always reassurance in this pattern of mine. The northern midwinter is an instinct for a spirit made of nightfire; I am the green flame in the skies where I dream and dance, it is the light I guide with to survive this bitter season.

With gentle gloved hands, I cradle each day I have left in this tiny Nordic town; astronomical twilight is falling now. The horizon is vanishing, so I will navigate with lantern and light; hope and soul; time and love.

ARCTIC CIRCLE OF FIRE

I throw my body back-first into freezing water,
a temporary break from swallowed heartache,
alive again. Scrambling to find balance on mossy
rocks, I race to the warmth of a wooden hut on the
shoreline of a northern lake. Twenty-two years old,
I sit in a sauna in the Arctic Circle with a
companion of mine, sprawling out on damp
planks. As I tilt my chin back to inhale the
humidity, I am enamoured with the visual of the
sweat and fresh water gleaming on our skin in the
fiery light.

I see my stories shine in this autumn moonlight; it
pushes against my ribcage as I struggle to decipher
how to best tell these tales.

This landscape, I have painted: gentle hills
filled with dark evergreens, laughter that
echoes across still water, two young artists at
the edge of the world. My oils are forged with
the fears that once chained me and the truths
I've earned from leaving them behind. I found
my brushes lodged in the back of my throat, I
coughed them up in the smoke of a fire
burning above as alike so within—I crave this
thrill, evolving with the polarity, stone blue
arctic skies and red-hot sauna coals. I am
addicted to the sting of my own heart's will,
so I will savor the aftertaste of the ghosts who
whisper through bitter boxed wine.

The land speaks

through my heart.

STORYTELLING

Let me bend time now, blur the lines between sentences, I write to silence chronology and all its dead. Existing between bliss and agony, I am *drawn* to abstraction—to be as we are, that is our humanity, that is our neutrality. Let connection flourish, let it be dampened with ink and paint and tears, let us wield the pain that follows, give in and *lean into*.

My spirit incarnates each ghost I summon, a chromatic apparation wayward to consistency; to paint with my heart is to learn my compatible mediums, ruining pieces of me to repair them.

This is how I create.

I am not sure myself what it is, should be, couldn't be, I breathe the comfort and serenity of it all; we are creation, creation is art.

How beautiful it is, to share such intensity in passion, to find imagination and hope in emotion—the human experience is ours to share between us and the world, we are just two liminality-addicted artists creating chapters of purpose in one larger novel.

LEAN INTO

12-10-2025

LEAN INTO

It is easier to fall into heartbreak's stiff arms, gentle now—close your eyes and let the pain take you in waves, your strongest days are yet to come. Resistance is the enemy of growth, for our greatest creation arrives in the wake of our destruction.

The dance of your fire burns hotter each time it flares, but this light will guide you to who you are meant to be. Raise your head, pull your sleeves back and *get up*—this is only the beginning.

Lean into me, rest your tired mind and I will hold your heart with grace—to know how much love you deserve, I will fight for it, take this blood of mine and paint your dreams to life.

—Milo

NIGHTFIRE

We ran outside with a blanket and threw ourselves
into a dusk-dewy meadow. With sides pressed
together, we stared at green fire above us, in us,
inside out, outside in. I left my body in that
moment; a ghost of myself, I am seeing the art we
are creating by simply existing.

Above, rivers of light laced a dark night. I wrapped
my fingers around his forearm and guided him to
point up at the paths of auroral ribbons.

We are a painting underneath the nightfire.

Author's Note

This collection began when I was a senior in high school, eventually growing to become a 40,000-word project paced down to the contents of this book. For the last five years, I have poetically recorded my journeys through landscape and lessons alike; I find a particular fascination with the intersectionality between the natural world, emotion, and memory. This book contains poetry that was written in Kansas, Colorado, Alaska, Yellowstone National Park, Finland, and Norway, all places I lived in from age eighteen to twenty-three.

I decided to publish my poetry at the foot of my creative gravestone; my answer to the artist's wrath I found walking through a cemetery in Oslo at midnight, in the snowy Nordic valley I am in right now.

I have worked to collide my ghosts into the one larger story told and illustrated within this one manuscript.

Reader, my wish is that you found understanding somewhere amidst these pages. At the end of the day, we are made human by our will to create and relate with ourselves, each other, and all the life surrounding us. The world is so much more than the cages of our own fears, trust me, I'd know. In an age where the arts face against digital silence, we find our humanity by the wisdom and experiences we share between ourselves and the Earth itself. I hope our art brought you joy, inspiration, and most importantly, hope itself in the ghosts that follow you, too.

Perseverance is the only force I am bound to, take this strength of mine and carry on, gently now.

— Milo

Author's Note

This collection began when I was a senior in high school, eventually growing to become a 40,000-word project parred down to the contents of this book. For the last five years, I have poetically recorded my journeys through landscape and lessons alike; I find a particular fascination with the intersectionality between the natural world, emotion, and memory. This book contains poetry that was written in Kansas, Colorado, Alaska, Yellowstone National Park, Finland, and Norway, all places I lived in from age eighteen to twenty-three.

I decided to publish my poetry at the foot of my creative gravestone; my answer to the artist's wrath I found walking through a cemetery in Oslo at midnight, in the snowy Nordic valley I am in right now.

I have worked to collide my ghosts into the one larger story told and illustrated within this manuscript.

Reader, my wish is that you found understanding somewhere amidst these pages. At the end of the day, we are made human by our will to create and relate with ourselves, each other, and all the life surrounding us. The world is so much more than the cages of our own fears; trust me, I'd know. In an age where the arts face digital silence, we find our humanity by the wisdom and experience we share between ourselves and the Earth. I hope our art brought you joy, inspiration, and most importantly, hope itself in the ghosts that follow you, too.

Perseverance is the only force I am bound to, take this strength of mine and carry on, gently now.

- Milo

Acknowledgements

To Joanna, Nicole, and all the teachers and professors who guided me to my writer's voice and taught me all I know about the natural world;

To Elrose and Kaitlyn, who cheered on Sauli & I in the creation process of this book, and their endless support for us and the WOG team as a whole;

To Mags, Tyler, Prue, and all the friends who have accompanied me on my adventures;

To Mom, Dad, and Aidan for always uplifting and encouraging my writing and artistic endeavors;

To Kristiina, for room & board in the far North, as well as for her spirit & inspiration;

To Alleycat, for always giving me a warm and welcoming space to work on my writing for countless hours;

To all the ghosts who have given me my toughest battles and taught me my greatest lessons.

THE WORLD OF

GARDIAN

Milo is a 23-year-old author, poet, and American-based naturalist. For over 10 years, he has dedicated to becoming a storyteller for the World of Gardian. He strives to uphold artistic kinship and ecological education through his writing.

Sauli is a Finnish artist invested in visual storytelling and efforts to combat catastrophic climate change. Humanity and whimsy are important, too.

We're still working on the second edition of *The Age of Scorpius*, don't worry!

www.ingramcontent.com/pod-product-compliance
Lightning Source LLC
Chambersburg PA
CBHW041219270326
41931CB00005B/117